Also by C. K. Williams

Lies (1969)
I Am the Bitter Name (1971)
With Ignorance (1977)
Sophocles' Women of Trachis (with Gregory Dickerson) (1978)
The Lark. The Thrush. The Starling.: Poems from Issa (1983)
Tar (1983)
Flesh and Blood (1987)
Poems 1963–1983 (1989)
The Bacchae of Euripides (1990)

A Dream of Mind

A DREAM OF MIND

Poems

C. K. WILLIAMS

Farrar, Straus and Giroux

New York

Copyright © 1992 by C. K. Williams
Printed in the United States of America
Published in Canada by HarperCollinsCanadaLtd
Designed by Cynthia Krupat
First published by Farrar, Straus and Giroux in 1992
First paperback edition, 1993

Library of Congress Cataloging-in-Publication Data
Williams, C. K. (Charles Kenneth).
    A dream of mind : poems / C. K. Williams. — 1st ed.
    I. Title.
  PS3573.I4483D74   1992   811'.54—dc20   92-2951 CIP

Some of these poems have appeared in the following
publications: "When" and "The Mirror" in *The New
Yorker*. "Helen" in *The American Poetry Review* and *The
Irish Review*. A signed, limited edition was also published
in November 1991 by Orchises Press of Alexandria,
Virginia. "Allies: According to Herodotus," "Chapter
Eleven," "Harm," "The Cautionary," "Pillow Talk," and
"Ethics" in *The Times Literary Supplement*. From the
sequence "A Dream of Mind," "History" first appeared in
Tikkun, "Room" and "The Knot" in *Antaeus*, and "The
Gap" in *The Threepenny Review*. "She, Though" first
appeared in *TriQuarterly*, a publication of Northwestern
University. "Signs" in *The Madison Review*, in a different
version, under the title "Soldiers." "Scar" and, from "A
Dream of Mind," "The Crime," "To Listen," and "The
Covenant" in *The Kenyon Review*." "Politics" and "The
Idyll" in *Phoebe*

ISBN 0-374-52376-2

for
Tex and Barbara
and
Lynn and Bob

Contents

1

2
Some of the Forms of Jealousy

3

4

A Dream of Mind

5

1

When

As soon as the old man knew he was actually dying, even before anyone
    else would admit it,
he wanted out of the business, out of the miserable game, and he told
    whoever would listen,
whenever they'd listen, wife, family, friends, that he'd do it himself but
    how could he,
without someone to help, unable to walk as he was, get out of bed or
    up from the toilet himself?

At first he'd almost been funny: "Somebody comes, somebody goes,"
    he'd said on the birth of a niece,
and one day at lunch, "Please pass the cream cheese," then, deadpan,
    "That's all I'll miss."
But now he's obsessed: "Why won't you help me?" he says to his children,
    ten times a day,
a hundred and ten, but what if such meddling's wrong, and aren't these
    last days anyway precious?

Still, he was wearing them down: "This is no fun," he said to a son
    helping him hobble downstairs,
and the son, knowing full well what he meant, dreading to hear what
    he meant, had to ask "What?"
so the old man, the biopsy incision still lumping the stubble of hair on
    the side of his skull,
could look in his eyes and say, if not as an accusation then nearly, "Death,
    dying: you know."

By then they knew, too, that sooner or later they'd have to give in, then
    sooner was over,
only later was looming, aphasiac, raving too late, so they held council
    and argued it out,
and though his daughter, holding onto lost hopes, was afraid, they decided
    to help him,

3

and told the old man, who said, "Finally, at last," and then to his
    daughter, "Don't be afraid."

On the day it would happen, the old man would be funny again: wolfing
    down handfuls of pills,
"I know this'll upset my stomach," he'd say, but for now he only asks
    how it will happen.
"You'll just sleep," he's told, and "That's great" is his answer: "I haven't
    slept for weeks."
Then "Great" again, then, serious, dry-eyed, to his weeping family: "Just
    don't tell me when."

The Vessel

I'm trying to pray; one of the voices of my mind says, "God, please help
me do this,"
but another voice intervenes: "How conceive God's interest would be to
help you believe?"

Is this prayer? Might this exercise be a sign, however impure, that such
an act's under way,
that I'd allowed myself, or that God had allowed me, to surrender to this
need in myself?

What makes me think, though, that the region of my soul in which all
this activity's occurring
is a site which God might consider an engaging or even an acceptable
spiritual location?

I thought I'd kept the lack of a sacred place in myself from myself,
therefore from God.
Is *this* prayer, recognizing that my isolation from myself is a secret I no
longer can keep?

Might prayer be an awareness that even our most belittling secrets are
absurd before God?
Might God's mercy be letting us think we haven't betrayed those secrets
to Him until now?

If I believe that there exists a thing I can call God's mercy, might I be
praying at last?
If I were, what would it mean: that my sad loneliness for God might be
nearing its end?

I imagine that were I in a real relation with God instead of just being
lonely for Him,
the way I'd apprehend Him would have nothing to do with secrets I'd
kept, from Him or myself.

I'd empty like a cup: that would be prayer, to empty, then fill with a
    substance other than myself.
Empty myself of what, though? And what would God deign fill me with
    except my own prayer?

Is this prayer now, believing that my offering to God would be what He'd
    offered me?
I'm trying to pray, but I know that whatever I'm doing I'm not: why aren't
    I, when will I?

Allies: According to Herodotus

"Just how much are you worth?" Xerxes asks Pythius, reputedly the richest
    man in Lydia,
at the entertainment Pythius was holding in his palace for Xerxes and
    his chiefs of staff.
"Exactly three million nine hundred and ninety-three thousand golden
    darics," Pythius answers,
"and all of it is yours, my humble contribution towards your glorious
    war against the Greeks."

Xerxes is pleased: since he's left Persia with his troops, only Pythius along
    their route
has offered hospitality without being compelled to; all this might indicate
    a welcome drift.
"Consider yourself my personal friend," he says to Pythius: "Keep your
    fortune, you've earned it,
and furthermore I'm awarding you another seven thousand darics of my
    own to round it off."

Later, as Xerxes is preparing to go on, an eclipse is sighted, which ir-
    rationally alarms Pythius,
but also encourages him to ask Xerxes for a favor. "Anything you want
    just ask," says Xerxes.
"I have five sons," Pythius replies, "and all of them are leaving to take
    part in your campaign.
I'm getting on: let me keep my eldest here, to help take care of me and
    see to my estates."

Xerxes is incensed. "You ungrateful scum," he snarls, "you have the gall
    to talk about your son,
when I myself, Xerxes himself, is going off to fight with all my sons and
    friends and relatives?
It would have pleased my ears if you'd offered me your *wife*, and thrown
    in your old carcass.

You saved yourself by your generosity the other night, but now you'll
    know a real king's rage."

Some ancients doubt Herodotus, but not in this; Xerxes, after all, angry
    at the Hellespont,
had it lashed and branded; we can trust therefore that near the moment
    when history begins,
Xerxes commanded that the beloved elder son of Pythius be brought to
    him and cut in half,
and that the halves be placed along the roadside for his army to march
    out towards Greece between.

Harm

With his shopping cart, his bags of booty and his wine, I'd always found
     him inoffensive.
Every neighborhood has one or two these days; ours never rants at you
     at least or begs.

He just forages the trash all day, drinks and sings and shadowboxes, then
     at nightfall
finds a doorway to make camp, set out his battered little radio and slab
     of rotting foam.

The other day, though, as I was going by, he stepped abruptly out between
     parked cars,
undid his pants, and, not even bothering to squat, sputtered out a noxious,
     almost liquid stream.

There was that, and that his bony shanks and buttocks were already stained
     beyond redemption,
that his scarlet testicles were blown up bigger than a bull's with some
     sorrowful disease,

and that a slender adolescent girl from down the block happened by right
     then, and looked,
and looked away, and looked at me, and looked away again, and made
     me want to say to her,

because I imagined what she must have felt, It's not like this, really, it's
     not this,
but she was gone, so I could think, But isn't it like this, isn't this just
     what it is?

The Insult

Even here, in a forest in the foothills of a range of mountains, lucent
    air, the purest dawn,
a continent and years away from where it happened, it comes back to
    me, simmering and stinging,
driving me farther down along the pathway to a hidden brook I hadn't
    realized was there.

The thrust came first, accurate, deft, to the quick, its impetus and rea-
    sonings never grasped.
Then my pain, my sullen, shocked retort, harsh, but with nothing like
    an equivalent rancor.
Then the subsiding: nothing resolved, only let slide; nothing forgiven,
    only put by.

The stream bends here under a bridge, its voice lifts more loudly from
    the rocks of its bed.
The quickly hardening light slants in over the tough, sparse wild grasses
    on the far hill.
Wind rattling the aspens; a hawk so tiny it seems almost a toy hovering
    in a socket of updraft.

Even now, I have no real wish to tell it, I know it so well why have to
    recite it again?
What keeps bringing us back to those fissures so tenaciously holding our
    furious suffering?
Are there deeper wounds in us than we know; might grief itself be com-
    munion and solace?

So many footprints crossing and recrossing the trail through the boulders
    edging the bank;
the swarms of apparently purposeless insects ticking their angular circuits
    over the water.
The song of the water, the mindless air, the hawk beyond sight, the
    inaudible cry of its prey.

Child Psychology

For Loren Crabtree and Barbara Cram

In that stage of psychosexual development called latency, when not that
      much, at least supposedly,
is going on—libido sleeps, the engrossing Oedipal adventure is forgotten
      for a time—
we were going somewhere and without telling him I took my father's
      keys and went outside to wait.
House, car, office keys: how proud I was to be the keeper of that weighty,
      consequential mass.
I stood there, tossing it from hand to hand, then, like my father, high
      into the air.
And then I missed, and saw it fall, onto the narrow grating of a storm
      sewer, and then in.

I gazed, aghast, down into those viscous, unforgiving depths, intestinal,
      malignant, menacing.
What happened? Had I dropped the keys on purpose? God no: I well
      knew my father's hand.
They'd just fallen, by themselves, that's what I'd say; no, say nothing,
      that was even better,
keep still, lips sealed, stoicism, silence—what other mechanism did I
      have beside denial?
Which is what I implemented when my father came to question me,
      and question me again.
Wholly taken in the burning ardor of my virtue, I was as innocent as
      Isaac, and as dumb.

Months pass, the doorbell rings, as always I'm the one to run to answer;
      a man is there,
he holds the long-forgotten ring of keys, my father's name, address, and
      number legible, intact.
I don't remember what men wore back then to muck about in filth for
      us, but it didn't matter;
the second I saw him I knew him—*the return of the repressed* . . . so
      soon, though, so very soon.

The shudderings I drove within were deafening; I couldn't bring myself
　　　to speak, but knew he would,
as I knew what he would say: "Is your father home?" He was, he was:
　　　how could he not be?

Chapter Eleven

As in a thousand novels but I'll never as long as I live get used to this
    kind of thing,
the guy who works as director of something or other in the business my
    friend owns and who,
I'm not sure why, we're out, my friend and I, for an after-work drink
    with, keeps kidding around,
making nice, stroking us, both of us, but of course mostly my friend,
    saying "Yes, boss, yes, boss,"
which is supposed to be funny but isn't because joke or no joke he's really
    all over my friend,
nodding, fawning, harking hard, and so intense it all is, with such edges
    of rage or despair—
is my friend letting him go? is his job as they say in that world, that hard
    world, on the line?—
that finally even my friend, who must have suspected something like this
    was going to happen
(why bring me then?), gets edgy, there are lapses, we all shift, then my
    friend says something,
"I don't feel great," something, "I have a headache," and, without think-
    ing, I'm sure without thinking,
it happens so quickly, the guy reaches, and, with the back of his hand,
    like a nurse or a mother,
feels my friend's forehead, as though to see if he has a fever, and my
    friend, what else? jerks back,
leaving the hand hung there in mid-air for a moment, almost saluting,
    almost farewelling,
until finally the poor man hauls the hand in, reels it back in, and does
    what with it?
Puts it for a moment lightly on the back of his head, lightly on his collar,
    the table, his drink?
All right, yes, the back of his head, lightly; lightly, his collar, the table,
    his drink.
But what does it matter anyway what the poor man does with his poor
    marooned hand?

Besides, he's fine now, we're all fine, it was all just a blink, the man's
folded his hands,
you'd think he was just saying grace or something, and probably nothing
happened at all,
you probably just blinked and drifted and imagined it all; if you asked
the man how he was,
what would he say, except "What do you mean?" and what would you
do but shut up and smile,
this isn't the *Death of a Salesman*, nobody here is going to turn into a
Gregor Samsa;
if you were him, wouldn't the last thing you'd want be for someone like
me to me-too you?
My friend beckons, the check comes on its little salver and my friend
stares down at it hard.
"I'm dead," he says finally. "I'm on such a short leash with the bank, I
can't make a dime."

The Loneliness

Not even when my gaze had gone unmet so long, starved so long, it
    went out of my control;
the most casual passing scrutiny would make my eyes, though I'd implore
    them not to,
scurry, slither, dart away to execute again their cowardly, abject ceremony
    of submission.

It was as though my pupils had extruded agonizing wires anyone who
    wanted to could tug.
What I looked at, what let approach me, had virtue only in so much as
    it would let me be,
let me hide further back within myself, let that horrid, helpless, sideways
    cringing stop.

Not even when my voice became so riddled with disuse my only recourse
    seemed to be to cry.
Some pointless pride, though, wouldn't let me: I'd ransack the layers of
    numb, resisting tissue,
but when I'd touch my cheeks they'd still be dry, even that benign release
    had been proscribed.

I'd think there might be something I could tell myself that would be
    equivalent to crying,
an idea or locution that would excavate a route through those impacted
    wells of desolation.
Thought hurt now, though; I couldn't concentrate: the most elementary
    logic lay beyond me.

Not even when, near sleep, it seemed somewhere in my mental boil my
    name was being called.
I'd reach out to hold the voice, then I'd realize that "name" and "call"
    were only symbols,
that some more painful aural stuff was solidifying in the echoing am-
    phitheater of my skull.

No wonder my fascination turned to those as lost as me, the drugged,
  the drunk, the mad.
Like ancient wounds they were, punctured with their solitude and sorrow,
  suppurating, stinking;
I'd recoil from what the soul could come to, but I knew within my soul
  that they were me.

My life, too, eluded me; I, too, learned to shun what of myself I saw in
  those around me.
No face now without its screen of categorical resistance, no glance un-
  tainted by denial.
I was being spoored by my imaginations; I felt guilt, and then remorse,
  as though I'd sinned.

I thought I'd come to know it then, when it began to turn on me, become
  its own exacerbation,
when the most unpremeditated look or smile or gesture, coming from it
  didn't matter who,
roused only rage in me, rejection, fire . . . I was close then, closer, but
  no, not even then.

By then, though, I was near the end; I'd never thought I would, but I
  was looking back,
almost apprehensive for the innocent I'd been, wondering if it all had
  been a romance,
if I might have really sanctioned all that hard annealing, and even then
  I hadn't understood.

When I knew, it was long after I imagined that I'd let it go; when I saw
  it come upon my children;
when I knew that they believed as I'd believed they'd never be sufficient
  to themselves again;
when I realized there was nothing I could do or say to help them: then,
  and only then.

Scar

As though the skin had been stripped and pulled back onto the skull like
    a stocking and soldered
too tightly so that it mottled to yellow and ocher, the pores and follicles
    thumbed out of the clay
by the furious slash of flame that must have leapt on her and by the
    healing that hurt her—

if it is healing that leaves her, age three, in a lassitude lax on her mother's
    broad lap,
bleak, weary, becalmed, what's left of her chin leaned heavily onto what's
    left of her fingers,
those knobs without nails, diminished, blunted, as though someone had
    hammered them thicker;

nares gone, ears gone, most of the dear lips gone so that your gaze is
    taken too deeply, terribly,
into the pool of the mouth as into a genital; the eyelids upper and lower
    wrinkled like linen,
the blood rims of the eyes too graphically vivid; harsh, tearless, porno-
    graphically red—

and you are supposed not to look or look and glance quickly away and
    not look at the mother,
who signs with a stone shoulder and eyes fixed to the child's white-gauze
    surgical cap
that if you do look you are cursed, if you do look you will and you well
    know it be damned.

Lascivious pity, luxurious pity, that glances and looks and looks twice
    and delivers the tear
and hauls out of the blind, locked caves of the breast these silent strangles
    of sobs
that ache but give something like tremulous whispers of sanctity back,
    psalms of gratification.

Lascivious pity, idle, despicable pity, pity of the reflexive half-thought
    holy thought
thinking the mindless threnody of itself once again: I watched, I couldn't
    not watch her,
as she so conscientiously, carefully wouldn't watch me; rapacious, pil-
    laging pity: forgive me.

2

Some of the Forms

of Jealousy

Signs

My friend's wife has a lover; I come to this conclusion—not suspicion,
    mind, conclusion,
not a doubt about it, not a hesitation, although how I get there might
    be hard to track;
a blink a little out of phase, say, with its sentence, perhaps a word or
    two too few;
a certain tenderness of atmosphere, of aura, almost like a pregnancy,
    with less glow, perhaps,
but similar complex inward blushes of accomplishment, achievement,
    pride—during dinner,
as she passes me a dish of something, as I fork a morsel of it off, as our
    glances touch.

My friend's manner, or his guise, is openness, heartiness and healthy
    haleness in all things;
the virtue of conviction, present moment, that sort of thing: it is his
    passion and his ethic,
so I don't know now if he knows or doesn't know, or knows and might
    be hiding it, or doesn't care.
He is hearty, open, present; he is eating dinner in the moment with his
    wife and old dear friend.
The wife, wifely, as she pours my wine and hands it to me looks across
    the glass's rim at me.
Something in the wifely glance tells me now she knows I know, and
    when I shyly look away,
reach across for bread and butter, she looks down at my hand, and up
    again: she is telling me
she doesn't care the least bit if I know or don't know, she might in fact
    wish me to know.

My friend is in the present still, taking sustenance; it's sustaining, good;
    he smiles, good.
Down below, I can just make out the engines of his ship, the stresses,
    creaks, and groans;

everything's in hand; I hear the happy workers at their chugging furnaces
and boilers.
I let my friend's guise now be not my guise but truth; in truth, I'm like
him, dense, convinced,
involved all in the moment, hearty, filled, fulfilled, not just with manner,
but with fact.
I ply my boilers, too; my workers hum: light the deck lamps, let the string
quartet play.

My friend's wife smiles and offers me her profile now; she is telling me
again: but why?
She smiles again, she glows, she plays me like a wind chime; I sit here
clanging to myself.
My friend doesn't seem to see me resonating; he grins, I grin, too, I flee
to him again.
I'm with him in his moment now, I'm in my mouth just as he's in his,
munching, hungrily, heartily.
My safe and sane and hungry mouth hefts the morsels of my sustenance
across its firmament.
The wife smiles yet again, I smile, too, but what I'm saying is if what
she means is so,
I have no wish to know; more, I never did know; more, if by any chance
I might have known,
I've forgotten, absolutely, yes: if it ever did come into my mind it's slipped
my mind.
In truth, I don't remember anything; I eat, I drink, I smile; I hardly even
know I'm there.

The Cautionary

A man who's married an attractive, somewhat younger woman conceives
a painful jealousy of her.
At first he's puzzled as to why he should brood so fretfully on her faith-
fulness or lack of it.
Their lovemaking is fulfilling: he enjoys it, his wife seems to, too, as
much as he does,
or, to his surprise (he's never had this experience before), maybe more
than he does.
When they married, it had seemed a miracle, he'd hardly been able to
believe his great luck:
the ease and grace with which she'd come to him, the frank, good-
humored way she'd touch him.
But now . . . it isn't that she gives too much meaning to sex, or exhibits
insufficient affection,
it's how *involved* in it she gets, so nearly oblivious, in a way he can never
imagine being.
He finds that he's begun to observe their life in bed with what he thinks
is a degree of detachment.
He sees himself, his blemishes, the paunch he can't always hide, then
her, her sheen, her glow.
Why, he asks, would such a desirable woman have committed herself
so entirely to such as him?
And, more to the point: why this much passion, these urgencies and
wants, this blind delight?
By a train of logic he can't trace to its source but which he finds chillingly
irrefutable,
he decides that it's not he himself, as himself, his wife desires, but that
she simply *desires*.
He comes to think he's incidental to this desire, which is general, un-
specific, without object,
almost, in its intensity and heat, without a subject: she herself seems
secondary to it,
as though the real project of her throaty, heaving passion was to melt
her mindlessly away.

Why would such need be limited to him: wouldn't it sweep like a search-
light across all maleness?

He can't help himself, he begins to put to the proof his disturbing but
compelling observations.

When they're out together, it's self-evident to him that every man who
sees her wants her:

all the furtive glances, behind, aside, even into surfaces that hold her
image as she passes.

It dawns on him in a shocking and oddly exciting insight that for so many
to desire her

some *signal* would have to be sent, not an actual gesture perhaps, nothing
so coarse as a beckoning,

but something like an aura, of eagerness, availability, which she'd be
subconsciously emitting.

Hardly noticing, he falls a step behind her, the better to watch her, to
keep track of her.

Then he realizes to his chagrin that his scrutiny might very well be
working on his wife.

In a sadly self-fulfilling prophecy, she might begin to feel vulnerable,
irritated, disconnected;

yes, alone, she must often feel alone, as though he, wretch that he is,
wasn't even there.

This is the last way he'd have thought that his obsession would undo
him, but why not?

A woman among admiring men is already in the broadest sense a potential
object of desire,

but a woman with a sharply heightened awareness of her most elementary
sexual identity,

as his wife by now would have, with this jackal, as he now sees himself,
sniffing behind her:

wouldn't she, even against her best intentions, manifest this in a primitive,
perceptible way,

and wouldn't men have to be aware, however vaguely, that some sexual
event was taking place?

Mightn't the glances she'd inspire reflect this, bringing an intriguing new
sense of herself,

and mightn't this make even more likely that she'd betray him in just
the way that he suspects?

Yes. No. Yes. He knows that he should stop all this: but how can he,
　　without going to the end?
The end might be just the thing he's driving them both towards, he can't
　　help himself, though,
he'll dissemble his fixations, but if there's to be relief, it will have to wait
　　till then.

Baby Talk

Willa Selenfriend likes Paul Peterzell better than she likes me and I am
    dying of it.
"Like" is what we say in eighth grade to mean a person has a secret crush
    on someone else.
I am dying of Willa liking Paul without knowing why she likes him more,
    or what it means.
It doesn't matter, Willa has insinuated cells of doubt in me, I already
    feel them multiplying,
I know already that a single lifetime won't be long enough to extirpate
    their progeny.
Willa likes Paul better than me but one summer day she'll come out to
    the park with me.
Why? Did she pity me? I don't care. We're there, we've walked, now
    we're resting on the grass.
Is this rest, though, to lie here, Willa so close, as lovely as ever, and as
    self-possessed?
I try, too, to calm myself, but the silence is painful; is this because Paul's
    in it, too?
Do I suspect it's that of which Willa's silence is composed? If so, of what
    is mine composed?
We lie there just a minute, or a year, the surgings and the pulsings in
    my heart and groin
are so intense that finally Paul's forgotten, only Willa's there with me,
    my docile longings.
Willa's turned towards me, her eyes are closed, I bring my face down
    closer, next to hers.
Astonishing that Willa should be in the visible with me, glowing in the
    world of pertinent form.
I move my lips towards hers, I can't resist, only this much, this gently,
    but then, no,
with one subtle shift, the mildest movement of the angle of her brow,
    Willa repositions us
so that my awkwardness makes absurd my plot of our participation in a
    mutual sensual accord.

With what humiliating force I have to understand I'd been suffering an
    unforgivable illusion;

I'd believed that for a little moment Paul had left us, but he'd been there
    all along,

with the unwavering omniscience of a parent, the power of what someday
    I'll call a conscience.

What had ever made me think I'd so easily obliterate him from the fraying
    dusk of childhood?

Weren't we contained in him, held in him; wouldn't fearful heart forever
    now falter in its flight?

The Question

The middle of the night, she's wide awake, carefully lying as far away as
    she can from him.

He turns in his sleep and she can sense him realizing she's not in the
    place she usually is,

then his sleep begins to change, he pulls himself closer, his arm comes
    comfortably around her.

"Are you awake?" she says, then, afraid that he might think she's asking
    him for sex,

she hurries on, "I want to know something; last summer, in Cleveland,
    did you have someone else?"

She'd almost said—she was going to say—"Did you have a *lover*?" but
    she'd caught herself;

she'd been frightened by the word, she realized; it was much too definite,
    at least for now.

Even so, it's only after pausing that he answers, "No," with what feeling
    she can't tell.

He moves his hand on her, then with a smile in his voice asks, "Did
    you have somebody in Cleveland?"

"That's not what I was asking you," she says crossly. "But that's what I
    asked *you*," he answers.

She's supposed to be content now, the old story, she knows that she's
    supposed to be relieved,

but she's not relieved, her tension hasn't eased the slightest bit, which
    doesn't surprise her.

She's so confused that she can't really even say now if she wants to believe
    him or not.

Anyway, what about that pause? Was it because in the middle of the
    night and six months later

he wouldn't have even known what she was talking about, or was it
    because he needed that moment

to frame an answer which would neutralize what might after all have
    been a shocking thrust

with a reasonable deflection, in this case, his humor: a laugh that's like
    a lie and is.

"When would I have found the time?" he might have said, or, "Who in Cleveland could I love?"

Or, in that so brief instant, might he have been finding a way to stay in the realm of truth,

as she knew he'd surely want to, given how self-righteously he esteemed his ethical integrities?

It comes to her with a start that what she most deeply and painfully suspects him of is a *renunciation.*

She knows that he has no one now; she thinks she knows there's been no contact from Cleveland,

but she still believes that there'd been something then, and if it was as important as she thinks,

it wouldn't be so easily forgotten, it would still be with him somewhere as a sad regret,

perhaps a precious memory, but with that word, renunciation, hooked to it like a price tag.

Maybe that was what so rankled her, that she might have been the object of his charity, his *goodness.*

That would be too much; that he would have wronged her, then sacrificed himself for her.

Yes, "Lover," she should have said it, "Lover, lover," should have made him try to disavow it.

She listens to his breathing; he's asleep again, or has he taught himself to feign that, too?

"No, last summer in Cleveland I didn't have a lover, I have never been to Cleveland, I love you.

There is no Cleveland, I adore you, and, as you'll remember, there was no last summer:

the world last summer didn't yet exist, last summer still was universal darkness, chaos, pain."

Meditation

You must never repeat this to him, but when I started seeing my guru
    was when I got pregnant.
I'm not bothered to think there's a connection—we'd been trying so
    long—but he would be.
He doesn't like my Baba, he says that he's repelled by him; I think he's
    really envious.
But why? Just because I believe in one person doesn't hurt my feelings for
    someone else.
You're supposed to give yourself to the guru, that's the whole idea, not
    that way, though.
He makes so much fuss: Baba is a fake, Baba is a pig; he says that I
    should leave him,
but he knows I won't: if he made me choose, I don't know what I'd do;
    and there's the baby.
When we made the baby, after my first visit to the ashram, I was so quiet
    inside, so serene,
as though I'd never been alive before; I felt Baba with me, just like when
    I met him.
I knew right away the pregnancy had taken, I knew I'd finally get my
    child; I was so happy.
I'm not lying to him, just not telling him; I can't, I won't. Don't you,
    either—promise!

Politics

They're discussing the political situation they've been watching evolve
    in a faraway country.
He's debating intensely, almost lecturing, about fanaticism and religion,
    the betrayal of ideals.
He believes he's right, but even as he speaks he knows within himself
    that it's all incidental;
he doesn't really care that much, he just can't help himself, what he's
    really talking about
is the attraction that he feels she feels towards those dark and passionate
    young men
just now glowing on the screen with all the unimpeachable righteousness
    of the once-oppressed.
He says that just because they've been afflicted isn't proof against their
    lying and conniving.
What he means is that they're not, because she might find them virile,
    therefore virtuous.
He says that there are always forces we don't see that use these things for
    evil ends.
What he means is that he's afraid that she might turn from him towards
    someone suffering,
or, as possible, towards someone who'd share with similar conviction her
    abhorrence of suffering.
He means he's troubled by how *sure* she is, how her compassions are so
    woven into her identity.
Isn't the degree to which she's certain of her politics, hence of her rightness
    in the world,
the same degree to which she'd be potentially willing to risk herself, and
    him, and everything?
Also, should she wish to justify an action in her so firmly grounded socio-
    ethical system,
any action, concupiscence, promiscuity, orgy, wouldn't it not only let
    her but abet her?
Sometimes he feels her dialectics and her assurance are assertions of some
    ultimate availability.

Does he really want someone so self-sufficient, who knows herself so
   well, knows so much?
In some ways, he thinks—has he really come to this?—he might want
   her knowing *nothing*.
No, not nothing, just . . . a little less . . . and with less fervor, greater
   pragmatism, realism.
More and more in love with her, touched by her, he still goes on, to his
   amazement, arguing.

Pillow Talk

Please try to understand, it was only one small moment, it didn't mean
    a thing, not really.
He was nice enough, but I didn't like him that much, I just felt, you've
    felt it, too, I'm sure,
a burden in my chest, as though I couldn't catch my breath, or get my
    heartbeat straight.
You know, I know you know: there's an ache in you, you want to make
    it stop, that awful flurrying;
you can't get back to where you used to like to be, everything is out of
    balance in you,
and you realize, even if you'd rather not, that the only way is with this
    other person,
you can't tell how you come to that conclusion, you feel silly, you hardly
    even know him,
he's almost not important anyway, he just represents release from all of
    it, a correction,
but you know that nothing else will get this settled in you, that you'll
    always be like this,
with this sense of incompletion, unless you act, even though you might
    not really want to,
so you go ahead and while it's happening you don't think of things like
    evil or betrayal,
you just want your inner world back in order so you can start to live your
    life again,
and then it's over, ended, you won't ever need him anymore, you realize
    it's finished, done.
I thought that you should know, that if you knew you'd understand: tell
    me, do you? Understand?

Ethics

The only time, I swear, I ever fell more than abstractly in love with
    someone else's wife,
I managed to maintain the clearest sense of innocence, even after the
    woman returned my love,
even after she'd left her husband and come down on the plane from
    Montreal to be with me,
I still felt I'd done nothing immoral, that whole disturbing category had
    somehow been effaced;
even after she'd arrived and we'd gone home and gone to bed, and even
    after, the next morning,
when she crossed my room undressed—I almost looked away; we were
    both as shy as adolescents—
and all that next day when we walked, made love again, then slept,
    clinging to each other,
even then, her sleeping hand softly on my chest, her gentle breath gently
    moving on my cheek,
even then, or not until then, not until the new day touched upon us,
    and I knew, knew absolutely,
that though we might love each other, something in her had to have the
    husband, too,
and though she'd tried, and would keep trying to overcome herself, I
    couldn't wait for her,
did that perfect guiltlessness, that sure conviction of my inviolable virtue,
    flee me,
to leave me with a blade of loathing for myself, a disgust with who I
    guessed by now I was,
but even then, when I took her to the airport and she started up that
    corridor the other way,
and we waved, just waved—anybody watching would have thought that
    we were separating friends—
even then, one part of my identity kept claiming its integrity, its non-
    involvement, even chastity,
which is what I castigate myself again for now, not the husband or his
    pain, which he survived,

nor the wife's temptation, but the thrill of evil that I'd felt, then kept myself from feeling.

The Mirror

The way these days she dresses with more attention to go out to pass the
    afternoon alone,
shopping or just taking walks, she says, than when they go together to a
    restaurant or party:
it's such a subtle thing, how even speak of it, how imagine he'd be able
    to explain it to her?
The way she looks for such long moments in the mirror as she gets ready,
    putting on her makeup;
the way she looks so deeply at herself, gazes at her eyes, her mouth,
    down along her breasts:
what is he to say, that she's looking at herself in ways he's never seen
    before, more *carnally*?
She would tell him he was mad, or say something else he doesn't want
    no matter what to hear.
The way she puts her jacket on with a flourish, the way she gaily smiles
    going out the door,
the door, the way the door slams shut, the way its latch clicks shut behind
    her so emphatically.
What is he to think? What is he to say, to whom? The mirror, jacket,
    latch, the awful door?
He can't touch the door, he's afraid he'll break the frightening covenant
    he's made with it.
He can't look into the mirror, either, that dark, malicious void: who
    knows what he might see?

The Call

When one of my oldest and dearest friends died and another friend called
    to console me,
I found myself crying—I hadn't thought I would—and said, "I didn't
    know I'd feel this badly."
Now, a year later, the second friend calls again, this time because his
    mistress has left him.
He's anguished, his voice torn; "I didn't know," he tells me, "that I'd
    feel this badly."
I'm shocked to hear him use precisely the words I had in my grief, but
    of course I understand.
There are more calls, and more, but in the end they all add up to much
    the same thing.
The mistress had warned him time and again, if not in so many words,
    that this might happen;
she'd asked him to leave his wife, he hadn't yet, but thought his honest
    oath to was in effect.
How was he to know that what he'd taken as playful after-intercourse
    endearments were threats?
Now that this terrible thing has happened, he's promised he'll really do
    it, but too late:
his beloved has found someone else, she's in love, no question now of
    beginning over.
At first my friend's desperation is sad to behold, his self-esteem is in
    harrowing decline;
decisiveness, or a lack of it, his lack of it, has become the key factor in
    his value system.
Gradually, though, he begins to focus on the new lover, on his insip-
    idness, his pitiful accomplishments.
There are flaws to this attack, though, because with each new proof of
    the other's shortcomings,
with each attempt to neutralize his effectiveness, my friend's self-blame
    becomes more acute.
Still, he can't say to himself, "Behold this giant competitor, this (Freud-
    ian) father of a man,"

so he keeps diminishing the other, which only augments his sense of the capriciousness of fate.

Then, to his relief (though he won't quite admit it), he finds sometimes he's furious at the woman.

How could she have done this? She'd known the risks he'd taken in doubling his affections,

shouldn't she simply have accepted his ambivalence and hesitation as a part of their relation?

And what about his wife; yes, some innocence, some purity has been transgressed there, too.

Her suspicions had been hot; she'd accepted his denials; wasn't that an offering to the mistress?

Aren't there violations, then, not just of his own good intentions but of his wife's generosity?

He's often hot with rage now, he doesn't even know at whom, but then he has to stop himself.

He doesn't want to blame the mistress *too* much, in case she should, despite all, come back,

and he doesn't want to hate his wife, who still doesn't know, or is even kinder than he thought.

So he keeps dutifully forgiving everyone, which throws the whole fault back on him again

and makes him wonder what kind of realignment could possibly redeem so much despair?

No, it's all ruined in advance, everything is stuck, the only thing he can do now is forget.

They're so degrading, these issues which can be resolved by neither consolation nor forgiveness.

No wonder my friend would cast his misery as mourning; no wonder, biting my tongue, I'd let him.

The Image

She began to think that jealousy was only an excuse, a front, for something
     even more rapacious,
more maniacally pathological in its readiness to sacrifice its own well-
     being for its satisfaction.
Jealousy was supposed to be a fact of love, she thought, but this was a
     compulsion, madness,
it didn't have a thing to do with love, it was perfectly autonomous, love
     was just its vehicle.
She thought: wasn't there a crazy hunger, even a delight, in how he'd
     pounced on her betrayal?
There hadn't even *been* betrayal until he'd made it so; for her, before
     that, it had been a whim,
a frivolity she'd gone to for diversion, it hadn't had anything to do with
     him, or them.
Her apologies meant nothing, though, nor her fervent promise of re-
     pentance, he *held* his hurt,
he cultivated, stroked it, as though that was all that kept him in rela-
     tionship with her.
He wanted her to think she'd maimed him: what was driving him to such
     barbarous vindictiveness?
She brought to mind a parasite, waiting half a lifetime for its victim to
     pass beneath its branch,
then coming to fully sentient, throbbing, famished life and without hes-
     itation letting go.
It must have almost starved in him, she thinks, all those years spent
     scenting out false stimuli,
all that passive vigilance, secreting bitter enzymes of suspicion, ingesting
     its own flesh;
he must have eaten at himself, devouring his own soul until his chance
     had finally come.
But now it had and he had driven fangs in her and nothing could contain
     his terrible tenacity.
She let the vision take her further; they had perished, both of them, there
     they lay, decomposing,

one of them drained white, the other bloated, gorged, stale blood oozing through its carapace.

Only as a stupid little joke, she thought, would anybody watching dare wonder which was which.

The Idyll

I just don't want to feel put down; if she decides she wants to sleep with
    someone, listen,
great, go ahead, but I want to know about it and I want the other guy
    to know I know;
I don't want some mother sliming in her sack, using her and thinking he's
    one up me.

She's always touching men, she sort of leans at them, she has to have
    them notice her,
want to grab her: it's like she's always telling me she's on the lookout for
    some stud,
some gigantic sex-machine who's going to get it on with her a hundred
    times an hour.

Once it really happened: she looked me in the eye and said, "I balled
    someone else last night."
Christ, I felt these ridges going up and down my jaw, I thought my teeth
    were going to break.
What'd I do? I took her home, we made out like maniacs. What else was
    I supposed to do?

Sometimes I wonder if I need it. I mean, she'll be coming onto somebody,
    as usual,
I'll want to crack her head for her, but if I think about it, I might get a
    buzz from it,
it must be what going into battle's like: sometimes I think going nuts from
    her is my religion.

I don't know if she fools around much now; I guess I'm not a whole lot
    into other women either.
The last time I was with another chick—she was a little knockout, too—
    I wasn't hardly there.
I realized who I wanted to be with was her. I turned off. Hell, is that
    how you get faithful?

The Silence

He hasn't taken his eyes off you since we walked in, although you seem
    not to notice particularly.
Only sometimes, when your gaze crosses his, mightn't it leave a very
    tiny *tuft* behind?
It's my imagination surely, but mightn't you be all but imperceptibly
    acknowledging his admiration?
We've all known these things; the other, whom we've never seen before,
    but whose ways we recognize,
and with whom we enter into brilliant complicities; soul's receptors tuned
    and armed;
the concealed messages, the plots, the tactics so elegant they might have
    been rehearsed:
the way we wholly disregard each other, never, except at the most casually
    random intervals,
let our scrutinies engage, but then that deep, delicious draft, that eager
    passionate appreciation . . .
I tell myself that I don't care, as I might not sometimes, when no rival's
    happened by,
but I do care now, I care acutely, I just wonder what the good would be
    if I told you I can see
your mild glances palpably, if still so subtly, furtively, intertwining now
    with his?
I'd only be insulting you, violating my supposed trust in you, belittling
    both of us.
We've spent so much effort all these years learning to care for one
    another's sensitivities.
In an instant that's all threatened; your affections seem as tenuous as
    when we met,
and I have to ask myself, are you more valuable to me the more that
    you're at risk?
Am I to you? It's degrading, thinking we're more firmly held together by
    our mutual anxiety.
If my desire is susceptible to someone else's valuations of its object, then
    what am I?

Can I say that my emotions are my own if in my most intimate affection
    such contaminations lurk?
Still, though, what if this time I'd guessed right, and what if I should try
    to tell you,
to try to laugh about it with you, to use our union, and our hard-earned
    etiquettes to mock him,
this intruder—look—who with his dream of even daring to attempt you
    would be ludicrous?
There would still be risks I almost can't let myself consider: that you'd
    be humoring me,
that the fierce intensity of your attraction to him would already constitute
    a union with him,
I'd be asking you to lie and doing so you'd be thrown more emphatically
    into his conspiracy;
your conniving with him would relegate me to the status of an obligation,
    a teary inconvenience.
This is so exhausting: when will it relent? It seems never, not as long as
    consciousness exists.
Therefore, as all along I knew I would, as I knew I'd have to, I keep still,
    conceal my sorrow.
Therefore, when you ask, "Is something wrong?" what is there to answer
    but, "Of course not, why?"

Soliloquies

1

Strange that sexual jealousy should be so much like sex itself: the same
    engrossing reveries,
the intricate, voluptuous pre-imaginings, the impatient plottings towards
    a climax, then climax . . .
Or, not quite climax, since jealousy is different in how uninvolved it is
    in consummation.
What is its consummation but negation? Not climax but relief, a sigh of
    resignation, disappointment.
Still, how both depend upon a judicious intermingling of the imaginary
    and the merely real,
and how important image is for both, the vivid, breath-held unscrolling
    of fugitive inner effigies.
Next to all our other minds, how pure both are, what avid concentration
    takes us in them.
Maybe this is where jealousy's terrific agitation comes from, because, in
    its scalding focus,
a desperate single-mindedness is imposed upon the soul and the sad,
    conditioned soul responds,
so fervently, in such good faith, it hardly needs the other person for its
    delicious fever.
Is there anything in life in which what is fancied is so much more intense
    than what's accomplished?
We know it's shadow, but licentious consciousness goes on forever man-
    ufacturing . . . fever.

2

The stupidity of it, the repetitiveness, the sense of all one's mental mech-
    anisms run amok.
Knowing that pragmatically, statistically, one's fantasies are foolish, but
    still being trapped.

The almost unmanageable foreboding that one's character won't be up
to its own exigencies.
Knowing one is one's own victim; how self-diminishing to have to ask,
"Who really *am* I, then?"
I am someone to be rescued from my mind, but the agent of my suffering
is its sole redemption;
only someone else, a specific someone else, can stop me from inflicting
this upon myself.
And so within myself, in this unsavory, unsilent solitude of self, I fall
into an odious dependency.
I'm like an invalid relying absolutely on another's rectitude; but the
desperate invalid, abandoned,
would have at least the moral compensation of knowing that he wasn't
doing this to himself;
philosophically, his reliance would be limited by the other's sense of
obligation, or its absence.
This excruciating, groundless need becomes more urgent, more to be
desired the more it's threatened,
while its denouement promises what one still believes will be an un-
imaginably luxurious release.

3

I try to imagine the kind of feeling which would come upon me if I really
were betrayed now.
How long would I remain in that abject state of mind? When would it
end? Am I sure it would?
What constitutes a state of mind at all? Certain chunks of feeling, of
pleasure or pain?
I postulate the pain, but can I really? My mood prevents it. Is that all I
am, then, mood?
Sometimes I feel firmly socketed within myself; other moments, I seem
barely present.
Which should I desire? Mightn't it be better not to feel anything if I'm
helpless anyway?
I try to reconceive the problem: I am he who will forgive his being
wronged, but can I know I will?

All my mind will tell me absolutely and obsessively is that its future isn't
    in my governance.
Might that be why the other's possible offense seems much more *rank*
    than mine would ever be?
My betrayal would be whimsical, benign, the hymen of my innocence
    would be quickly reaffirmed.
Hers infects, contaminates, is ever the first premeditated step of some
    squalid longer term.
I would forgive, but suspect that she might already be beyond forgiveness:
    whose fault then?

4

What would be the difference? The way jealousy seeps into my notions
    of intention and volition,
the annihilating force it has: mightn't it be grounded in the furies of more
    radical uncertainty?
That nothing lasts, that there's no real reason why it doesn't last, and
    that there's death,
and more maddening still that existence has conjectured possibilities of
    an after-death,
but not their certainty, rather more the evidence that any endlessness is
    mental fiction.
And that there might be a God, a potentially beloved other who *would*
    know, this, and everything,
who already has sufficient knowledge of our fate to heal us but may well
    decide not to do so.
How not rage, how, in love, with its promises of permanence, the only
    answer to these doubts,
not find absurd that this, too, should suffer from foreboding, and one so
    mechanically averted?
Might jealousy finally suggest that what we're living isn't ever what we
    think we are?
What, though, would more require our love, our being loved, our vow
    of faithfulness and faith?
And what would more compel that apprehensive affirmation: *I'll love you
    forever, will you me?*

3

She, Though

Her friend's lover was dying, or not "friend," they weren't that yet, if
    they ever really were;
it was another girl she'd found to share the studio she'd rented in an old
    commercial building.
Both of them were painters, the other serious, hardworking, she floun-
    dering and unconfident.
She gave you the feeling people fresh from art school often do that the
    painter's life
would be just fine except for all those hours you had to put in with the
    bothersome canvas.
"Lover" isn't quite the right word, either: the couple were too young,
    "boyfriend" would be better,
although, given the strenuousness of their trial, the more grownup term
    could well apply.
He was twenty-three or -four, a physicist who'd already done his doctorate
    and published papers;
he had cancer of the brain; it had only recently been diagnosed but the
    news had all been bad.
I forget exactly how I met them: there weren't that many writers or artists
    in our city then,
we mostly knew each other, even if our fellowship seemed more grounded
    in proximity than sympathy.
She and I, I suppose I should say, once almost had a thing; she asked
    me to sit for her,
and when she'd posed me and was fussing with her charcoal, I understood
    why I was really there.
I was surprised; though we'd known each other for a while we were casual
    friends at best,
we'd never expressed attraction for each other, and I remember feeling
    sometimes that she resented me.
I had a reputation as a worker, even if I hadn't published anything except
    some book reviews
and a criticism of an art show, but she may have felt I had more prestige
    than I should have.

I had nothing particularly against her; maybe the tenuousness of her
    involvement in her work
and what it represented to me of myself made her less attractive than she
    might have been.
I distrusted her, wasn't sure why she wanted me, but wasn't anyway about
    to get in bed.
Her signaling was pretty raw: she'd take my head in her hands to move
    me to a new position,
then hold me longer than she had to, and she'd look intently *in* my eyes
    instead of at them.
Finally she just said, "Let's do it," but I turned her down, in a way which
    at the time
I thought was very bright but which may certainly have had to do with
    how badly things turned out.
I told her that I liked her but that I could only sleep with girls I loved,
    really loved.
She accepted my refusal in the spirit I'd hoped she would, as an example
    of my inner seriousness,
and as also having to do—through I don't recall what track—with my
    dedication as an artist.
That dedication, or obsession, or semblance of obsession, counted for
    much in those days.
For most of us it was all we had, struggling through our perplexed,
    interminable apprenticeships.
We were trying to create identities as makers and as thinkers, and that
    entailed so much.
I never realized until lately just how traumatic the project of my own
    self-remaking was.
I wreaked such violence on myself; the frivolous, not unsuccessful ado-
    lescent I had been
had to be remolded from such contradictory clues as I could find into a
    wholly other person.
I'd been an *athlete*, for heaven's sake, I'd been a party boy, I hung out,
    I drank, I danced:
one New Year's Eve I'd set out to kiss a hundred girls, and nearly had;
    that kind of thing.
Now who was I? Someone sitting hours on end going crazy looking at
    an empty piece of paper.

Everything I'd learned in college seemed garbled and absurd: I knew
nothing about anything.
All I understood was that I wasn't ready for this yet, that I'd have to reach
some higher stage
before I'd have the right to even think that I was someone who could
call himself a poet.
We must have all felt more or less like that, though it seemed important
never to admit it.
"Morally perfect yourself, then you'll write a poem," I read somewhere
not long ago: is it true?
I don't think I know yet, I surely didn't then, but that was what we'd
somehow come to,
a mix of saint and genius, neither of which we ever in our wildest ravings
dreamed we'd be.
Maybe that was why we liked extremities so much, and mental dramas;
we spoke forever about *limits*,
things like microcosm-macrocosm, or the way the solar system and atomic
model seemed to match:
probably we thought that, on that wide a scale, we'd at least be sure of
being *somewhere.*
We loved it when things went so far they turned into their opposites; the
courteous criminal,
the rake who in his single-minded lust achieves a sanctity, the cabalist
obscene with bliss.
There were always remnants of religion in our schemes; somehow from
the mishmash of our education
we'd decided that you didn't practice art for its own sake or even to be
competent or famous;
it was all supposed to be a part of a something that would lift you to
another realm,
another mode of being, where you'd attain the "absolute"—a word we
loved—along with "mystic."
But there was even more than that; art was going to be the final word
on all else, too:
morality, philosophy, religion; if there was a God, wasn't He the God of
Dante or Bach,
rather than a theologian's or a prophet's, unless they dreamed their vi-
sions, too, in poetry?

51

When we thought of social issues or of politics, it was always with as
audacious an immoderation.
"Justice" meant the universe of justice; the ideal, platonic shape, some-
thing in your soul
that mirrored an imaginary, perfect state, at which the particulars of real
life could only hint.
History for us was the history of arts and letters, anything of moment was
attached to that.
So young we were; we had theories about everything, life, the soul: Did
art spring from neurosis?
Was its insanity redemptive? Were you damned by art, exalted? It all
depended on the day.
But being young wasn't the whole problem; there was moral character
to be considered, too.
That girl, for instance, in that enormous studio: it irritated me the way
she'd waste her time,
puttering, reading magazines; she spent more effort sending slides to
galleries than painting.
She'd been in some group exhibitions—she wasn't without talent—now
she'd convinced herself
that being "professional" meant not picking up a brush unless a dealer
promised you a show.
I knew all that was posturing, self-deception, sham; I knew from what I
went through myself
how repugnant working was when you didn't know if there was ever going
to be a recompense.
I don't mean to make light of it, what we were trying to do was hard,
and not just the work,
in some ways that was easy: what was really difficult was waiting for the
labor to begin;
you had to tell yourself every minute that you did it why you did and
what it was for.
So little really happened, and no one but a friend or two even noticed
what you were doing.
The dropout rate among us was impressive: over time so many drifted
off, some to law school,
some into endless therapies; a black sculptor began to drink and disap-
peared into the ghetto;

someone else became an "art consultant," choosing prints and paintings
for corporate boardrooms.

It did seem easier for some, though; some were seen as having been
successful from the start.

I suppose it had to do with confidence; they weren't necessarily the ones
who'd won the prizes,

but they seemed certified, legitimized, they had clues about their ultimate
trajectories;

you felt they'd freed themselves from thinking they were being *watched*,
those chosen few,

they were on their own and, though they hadn't done much yet, were
envied and looked up to.

What happens to those younger masters isn't always happy; maybe that
much unquestioning admiration,

that much carrying of so many other people's hopes, even at that level,
isn't good for you.

Also, when everyone's that young, there's much misreading of charisma
and eccentricity as talent.

Some, anyway, would turn out to have the gift, but not enough of what
you could call the *cunning*,

the kind of objectivity artists seem to need to keep their work evolving
in meaningful ways.

They'd find a mode of doing what their gift had offered them, then stay
with it too long,

and find later that they'd used it up and gotten stuck in some too flashy
segment of themselves.

Others would have the cunning, and the drive it seemed to go with, but
too much of it;

they'd become impatient, and move off to something close to art—usually
involving money—

to which they'd bring their ingenuity and energy, becoming rich or
celebrated, but so what?

She, I don't have to say, wasn't one of the elect, no more than I'd dare
claim I was.

The other girl may have been; if so, she controlled the arrogance it
sometimes went with.

The boyfriend for all we knew was a genius; we had to take his mysterious
accomplishments on faith.

He was brilliant enough in conversation, at any rate, and had an attractive
   calm about him.
In the face of his illness, and though no one dared speak of it, his at
   least possible death,
the two of them had evolved one of those surprising complicities of
   resignation and acceptance
which can take the most unexceptional people at such times, and they
   were hardly unexceptional.
They had an admirably mature relationship; they respected and encour-
   aged one another's work,
and were solicitous towards each other in gentle, complicated ways the
   rest of us found heartening.
But with all that, the dignity they seemed committed to achieving now
   was of another order.
For one thing, there was no denial in it, no trying to behave more fittingly
   before the facts.
They stayed mostly to themselves, and worked; if they did go anywhere,
   to an opening, say,
they left early, refusing to let anything intrude on their resolute and by
   now ennobling composure.
The rest of us must have been a little awed; being with them was like
   being with a movie star.
We may have been excited, too, and secretly inspired, but all they seemed
   to want from us
was that we act as though nothing unusual was happening, and we were
   all too happy to comply.
She, though, once she'd found out about it—the girl apparently at first
   had kept it from her—
wasn't taking anything so calmly, wasn't having any of this stoicism, this
   holding back.
I don't know how, but she was all at once their chum, their confidante,
   their social secretary.
She was blazing with consideration for them, some unsuspected energy
   had been released in her.
She dropped her painting altogether now, and did good deeds for them
   instead: she was everywhere,
organizing quiet dinners, getting people to throw parties; she even once
   promoted a recital,

which was supposed to give some of our musicians an opportunity to
play but which she turned—

and not in an unpleasantly pretentious way—into an elegant soiree and
cocktail honoring them.

They became, in fact, as she took over, the unofficial guests of honor
everywhere they went.

They hardly seemed to notice, though, and to hardly notice her; she was
like a stage director,

rushing back and forth behind the scenes, keeping all the action moving
unobtrusively along,

except it wasn't the audience which was supposed to be oblivious of all
the cable-hauling,

the changing sets and lighting, but the innocent creatures out on the
apron of the stage.

I often wondered, considering what they seemed to have wanted before
she started in on that,

whether they were ever bothered by her benevolent chicanery; they didn't
appear to be.

They could have stopped her, but their sorrow may have been more
oppressive than we knew;

maybe there was something that they needed after all, maybe it was just
that much attention.

Or it could all have been just another factor to be balanced in their
brilliant equation,

the way one of their mother's clutching a tissue to an irrepressible tear
would have been.

If they didn't have a problem with her machinations, though, I did; I
found it all depressing.

I thought I knew what she was up to—a naked compensation for her
failures at the easel—

and I began to stay away from functions she was overseeing, which meant
most of them by now.

I just kept to myself more, even if it meant afflicting myself with still
more loneliness,

a loneliness the opposite of what I found in books, where you went off
on your holy pilgrimage,

enriched yourself with arcane meditations on the universe, and then
produced your masterpiece.

My masterpiece, if I still could have a fantasy of such a thing, seemed
    more buried every day
beneath the layers of confusion, uncertainty, and mental maladroitness
    to which I was so susceptible.
I don't remember what finally brought me to the party where I saw the
    three of them again.
It was just a night at someone's house; everyone was there, I was glad to
    be there, too,
hearing other people's voices, breathing other people's breath, feeling
    ordinary human warmth.
The young man still looked well enough, the two of them were sitting
    at the piano, whispering.
She was near them; when she saw me, she came over, she was glad to
    see me, where had I been?
There was something she'd been wanting to ask me; no, not right now,
    wait, later on.
I couldn't conceive what question she might have for me, but I'd been
    by myself so much
that any contact was intriguing, and besides, she looked, with her new
    glow of purpose, quite enchanting.
As the party swirled on, I watched her; it was remarkable how she'd
    involved herself with them.
I'd never thought of her as subtle but I had to recognize how much
    intelligence she had for this.
She was always near them, but never overbearingly so; she was just
    available to them,
they were always in a triangle with her, as though she possessed some
    benign, proprietary power.
She'd bring them drinks and sandwiches, lead people over to them, lean
    down to listen, laugh.
It seemed natural when she'd lightly touch the lover's shoulder, or stroke
    the girl's hair.
Later on, I caught her hand and led her to the bedroom; what had she
    been going to ask?
What she asked was if I knew anything to read on death; could I rec-
    ommend a book on death.
At first I didn't understand what she was saying, I couldn't register it, get
    it down.

What? "You've read a lot of books," she said. "I need one to give to
somebody who's dying."
She said it quietly, she was serious, almost solemn, but she was looking
at my eyes this time.
"Something to comfort them," she added with conspiratorial intensity,
"in their ordeal."
I don't remember what I answered, if I did—I may have said they're all
on death, all books,
I still believed it sometimes in those days, it sometimes seemed the core
of my aesthetic code.
What I'm hearing now is "Timor mortis conturbat me"—"The fear of
death is killing me"—
but what I remember thinking then, with a desperate conviction, was
that she'd beaten me:
she'd held her grudge this long, and then attacked, prevailed, and won
our little agon.
By assuming, or making believe that she assumed, I'd be so unaware of
something of such moment,
she'd let me know I was an outcast among outcasts, subtracted from what
society I had, a pretender,
and by turning my own medium against me, showing how absurd it
would have been for me to think
that writing could heal or solace real grief, she'd proved that my preten-
sions were a farce.
I think I was amazed that she'd have used her own good deeds to get at
me, but more importantly,
I knew she'd touched some truth, and that something in me had been
undermined so profoundly
that as I turned from her, although of course I wouldn't let her know, I
must have almost staggered.
I think I doubted even then, though, how much my psychic storm really
had to do with her.
I knew she didn't hate me *that* much, and that what had happened to
us wasn't very deep.
No, it wasn't me she'd hated and wanted vengeance from, it was *art*; I
was just the medium,
a handy means to rebel against art, to degrade it, express how much she
despised it.

She'd chosen me to use—and this *had* hurt—because she knew I knew
     I wasn't really pure.
All my narcissism, all the juvenile self-indulgence that had let me think
     that as I was
I could still be an initiate in art's exalted realm, no matter how I lied
     and twisted my identity,
she'd long ago intuited, and finally struck with, and she may have even
     guessed—I hope not—
that in this moment I was living out what in turning to a life by art I'd
     been trying to evade.
I don't think I cared if she was taking satisfaction from my turmoil, she
     didn't matter anymore.
I beheld myself, and I was mortified, not because of anybody else's ideas
     or norms or values,
but for my own, all I'd studied and prepared for, which had suddenly
     become shameful to me.
"You must change your life": I knew Rilke's line already, now I had a
     hint of how it happened.
It's not easy to remember how much of what I later came to understand
     revealed itself that evening:
a mass of sad intention was set under way in me I've spent all these years
     trying to enact.
Right then I was most likely struck by just the wrongness of how I'd so
     far conceived my task.
I'd believed that art was everything, the final resolution of all my insecurity
     and strivings.
Now I realized that in attempting to create a character in art, someone
     who would live for art,
I'd turned away from something in myself, some lapse I hadn't glimpsed,
     and, more shocking still,
I knew that architecture, poetry, and painting weren't the self-containing
     glories I'd imagined,
but that they, too, could have evasions lurking in them, grievous cosmic
     flinchings from reality.
Art wasn't everything, nothing could be everything, but more crucially,
     art *needed* you:
I knew now that if you hated art, as she did, that was what you hated in
     it, that responsibility,

58

not to making up a self which might someday be worthy of ecstasy or
fame, but to art itself,

to the negating force it could become unless you understood what its
decisive limits were.

The power, the willed resolve I'd believed you needed for your work, I
knew now were elementary,

that arduous and obscure responsibility was what mattered most, and I
intuited, and *knew*,

that what it consisted of was a concern, for all of us, for every human
being: one by one.

The forms and substances were incidental, *we* were form and substance;
subject, object, reason.

"You must change your life." I knew then, or began to know, that what
art needed at the end

was an acceptance of what's muddled and confused in us, what's broken
by our lives and living.

To love art meant to love our errors; what we owed art was ourselves and
our imperfect world.

"Timor mortis conturbat me." "You must change your life." I was left
with my forbidding mottoes,

my attempts to overcome my unconfidence and indolence, and every
day my sorry stabs at poems.

Whether I used well what I learned that night, or if it changed me, how
am I to know?

Can we ever say in all good conscience we've really changed? We only
have our single story.

In mine, the physicist, the young man, the boy—what else would I think
he was by now?—

the poor boy dies sooner even than predicted; this all takes place in just
some months.

The boy dies, the girlfriend moves away; I see her work reviewed, years
later, in the *Times*;

they loved her: she was praised especially for her "mastery of expression":
good for her.

She—how specify her now? my antagonist? my demon other? the an-
tithesis in my groping dialectic?—

she drops from sight: I forgave her, but never heard another breath about
her, and never wanted to.

4

A Dream of Mind

for Adam Zagajewski

The Method

A dream of method first, in which mind is malleable, its products as
    revisable as sentences,
in which I'll be able to extract and then illuminate the themes of being
    as I never have.
I'm intrigued—how not be?—but I soon realize that though so much
    flexibility is tempting—
whole zones of consciousness wouldn't only be reflected or referred to,
    but embodied, as themselves,
before the sense-stuff of the world is attached to them, adulterating and
    misrepresenting them—
I have only the sketchiest notion of how to incorporate this exotic and
    complicated methodology,
and when I try, something in my character resists manipulating elements
    of mind so radically.
Imagine being offered an instrument to play that violated all your previous
    aesthetic norms,
with a fleshy, tender, sensitive component, crudely sewn or soldered to
    an innocently inorganic,
and a shape that hinted at the most contradictory techniques—brute
    force, a delicate dexterity.
You know you're supposed to draw this hybrid to your breast, to try to
    coax from it its music,
but under the tension of so many formal contradictions, what actually
    would you bring forth?
Isn't this like that? I'd be dreaming dreams of dreams, hammering out
    ideas of dreams:
wouldn't anything I'd come up with have to be a monstrous mix of
    substance and intention?
Making something out of nothing; surely more than matters of order or
    proportion are at stake.
I feel myself go cold now, taken by a clarity that makes me ask if I'm
    not already in the dream,
if I'm not merely being tempted by it, in the sense that one is tempted
    by an ill desire.

What if all this theory's the equivalent of nightmare, its menace mas-
    querading as philosophy?
Can mind contort itself so recklessly and not endanger its most basic links
    to common sense?
I dream a dream of method, comprehending little of the real forces or
    necessities of dream,
and find myself entangled in the dream, entrapped, already caught in
    what the dream contrived,
in what it made, of my ambitions, or of what it itself aspired to for its
    darker dreaming.

Shadows

They drift unobtrusively into the dream, they linger, then they depart,
        but they emanate, always,
an essence of themselves, an aura, of just the frequency my mind needs
        to grasp and contain them.
Sometimes, though, the identity that I sense there, the person I feel
        intimated or implied,
is so fluid and changes so rapidly and dramatically that often I hardly
        know who I'm with.
Someone is there, then they're someone from another moment of my
        life, or even a stranger.
At first I find such volatile mutability surprisingly less agitating than I'd
        have thought,
probably because these others brought and taken away by the dream
        manifest such careless unconcern.
Before long, though, I feel apprehensive: I find that whenever someone
        in the dream changes,
I subtly alter who I am as well, so as to stay in a proper relation with
        this new arrival
who may already be somebody else, someone for whom the self I've come
        up with is obsolete.
Suddenly I'm never quite who I should be; beset by all this tenuous
        veering and blurring,
my character has become the function of its own revisions; I'm a bystander
        in my own dream.
Even my response to such flux is growing unstable; until now I've con-
        sidered it speculatively,
but what says I'm not going to stay in this epistemologically tremulous
        state forever?
I find I'm trying to think how to stop this, but trying to think in dream
        means, as always,
trying to *do*, and what do now with this presence moving towards me,
        wavering, shifting,
now being itself, now another, webbed now in the shadows of memory,
        now brilliant, burning?

Am I to try to engage it, or turn back to myself to steel myself in a more
   pure concentration?
Even as I watch, it transfigures again; I see it, if it is it, as through ice,
   or a lens.
I feel a breath touch me now, but is it this breath I feel or someone's I
   haven't met yet,
is it a whisper I hear or the murmur of multitudes sensing each other
   closer within me?
How even tell who I am now, how know if I'll ever be more than the
   field of these interchangings?

Vocations

Blocks of time fall upon me, adhere for a moment, then move astonish-
        ingly away, fleeting, dissolving,
but still I believe that these parcels of experience have a significance
        beyond their accumulation,
that though they bear no evident relation besides being occasionally
        adjacent to each other,
they can be considered in a way that implies consequence, what I come
        to call the dream's "meaning."
Although I can't quite specify how this ostensible meaning differs from
        the sum of its states,
it holds an allure, *solutions* are implied, so I keep winding the dream's
        filaments onto its core.
The problem is that trying to make the recalcitrant segments of the dream
        cohere is distracting;
my mind is always half following what happens while it's half involved
        in this other procedure.
Also, my ideas about meaning keep sending directives into the dream's
        already crowded circuits,
and soon I'm hard put keeping the whole intractable mechanism moving
        along smoothly enough
to allow me to believe that at least I'm making a not overly wasteful use
        of my raw materials.
Although, doesn't the notion of "use" seem questionable, too? Use
        how, and to what end?
To proliferate more complexities when I haven't come to terms with those
        I've already proposed?
Mightn't all of this be only a part of the mind's longing to be other or
        more than it is?
Sometimes I think I'd be better off letting the dream make its own way
        without butting in so,
but no, I understand the chaos I might wreak if I left off these indispens-
        able cohesions.
How depressing dream can feel now, nothing in it can move, everything
        is suspended, waiting,

or, worse, not waiting, going on as it's always gone on but with such
fearful, timid resolve
that I begin to wonder if all that keeps me going is my fear of randomness,
regression, chance.
It doesn't matter anymore: whatever dream meant once, whatever it might
come to mean,
I know the only way I'll ever finish with this anguish is to understand it,
and to understand
was what the dream promised, and what, with all its blundering hopes,
it promises still.

The Solid

Although I'm apparently alone, with a pleasant but unextraordinary feel-
    ing of self-sufficiency,
I know I'm actually a part of a group of people who for reasons the dream
    never makes clear
are unavailable to any of my senses, though I'm always aware of the
    pressure of their presence.
No matter what else I'm doing, no matter how scant the attention I pay,
    I know they're there,
only my response to being in relation with beings I can only imagine
    alters now and again.
Usually I'm comforted: this intuition seems to impart to the dream such
    stability as it has.
Immersed with my mysterious companions in an enormous, benign,
    somehow consoling solid,
all that's required is that I not carelessly set jolts out into that sensitive
    bulk of otherness.
At other, nearly simultaneous moments, I feel signals sent, intentionally
    or not, I can't tell,
which arrive to my consciousness as an irritation, almost an abrasion of
    the material of thought.
In some far corner of dream, someone wants, needs, with such vehement,
    unreasonable fervor,
that even from here I'm afflicted with what I can only believe is an
    equivalent chagrin.
I try to think of ways to send back if not reassurance then an acknowl-
    edgment of my concern,
but I realize this would require not only energy and determination but
    a discernment, a delicacy,
the mere thought of which intimidates me, reinforcing the sense I have
    of my ineffectiveness.
I begin to be afraid then, the dream is deteriorating; how vulnerable I
    am in my very connections.
Don't my worst anxieties rise out of just such ambiguous feelings of
    communion and debt?

I'm suddenly swamped, overwhelmed in these tangles of unasked-for
   sympathies and alliances.
Always then, though, through an operation whose workings I'm never
   forced to explain to myself,
I'm released, the limits of my selfhood are reestablished, the nascent
   nightmare subsides,
and I'm able to reassume the not-incongruous sense of being alone and
   with so many others,
with nothing asked of me more than what any reasonable dream needs
   for its reasonable dreaming,
and the most minor qualms as to what I may have traded for my peace
   of mind, and what lost.

The Charge

An insistence in dream on a succession of seemingly urgent but possibly
  purposeless tasks
to be executed for no evident reason beyond the tautological one that
  dream says they must.
The nature of these undertakings is unclear, imprecise, they can even
  change definition,
I can never find more than the most ambiguous grounds to justify my
  obsession with them.
It seems sometimes that far away in the past of the dream a shameful
  error was committed,
and that these obligations are only my share of a more general rectification
  or atonement.
Often I can't tell if what I'm doing is by any sane measure what I'm
  supposed to be doing,
or whether all my efforts are the groundwork for yet another, still more
  illogical dream.
I'm never unaware either that I'm squandering time; this undermines my
  self-assurance still more,
so, the dream still driving me through it, me still helplessly driving myself
  through the dream,
I begin to think that persisting in this will put me into a state of such
  unmanageable consternation
that everything in me will simply go awry, leaving me tearing at myself
  in rages of frustration.
How long this has been under way, I can't tell; forever, it seems, all the
  time of the dream,
but maybe because I've looked back now, it comes to me that even should
  these needs be satisfied,
their compulsions slaked, it won't have been my doing: dream will just
  have pitied me,
given me surcease, not the satisfaction I'd anticipated despite all, but
  deflection and distraction.
All I'm left to hope for is that something other than nostalgia or regret
  awaits me,

that I won't end up longing for my labors, yearning for the solaces of
      goals I'd never grasped,
trying to remember when the dream of finishing what can't be finished
      ended, or if it did.

The Crime

Violence in the dream, violation of body and spirit; torment, mutilation, butchery, debasement.

At first it hardly feels real, there's something ceremonial in it, something of the dance.

The barbarisms seem formulaic, restrained, they cast a stillness about them, even a calm.

Then it comes once again, the torment, the debasement, and I have to accept that it's real.

Human beings are tearing each other to pieces, their rancor is real, and so is their pain.

Violence in the dream, but I still think—something wants me to think —there are *reasons*:

ideas are referred to, ideals, propositions of order, hierarchies, mores, structures of value.

Even in dream, though, I know it's not true, I know that if reasons there are, they're ill reasons.

Even in dream, I'm ashamed, and then, though I'm frightened, I steel myself and protest.

I protest, but the violence goes on, I cry out, but the pain, the rage, the rancor continue.

Then I suddenly realize I've said nothing at all, what I dreamed was spoken wasn't at all.

I dreamed I protested, I dreamed I cried out: I was mute, there was only an inarticulate moan.

What deceived me to think I'd objected when really I'd only cowered, embraced myself, moaned?

My incompetent courage deceived me, my too-timid hopes for the human, my qualms, my doubts.

Besides the suspicion perhaps that the dream doesn't reveal the horror but draws it from itself,

that dream's truth is its violence, that its pity masks something I don't want to find there.

What I hear now in the dream is the dream lamenting, its sorrow, its fear, its cry.

Caught in the reasons of dream, I call out; caught in its sorrow, I know who I hear cry.

Shells

Shells of fearful insensitivity that I keep having to disadhere from my
     heart, how dream you?
How dream away these tireless reflexes of self-protection that almost define
     heart
and these sick startles of shame at confronting again the forms of fear the
     heart weaves,
the certitudes and the hatreds, the thoughtless fortifications of scarred,
     fearful self?
How dream you, heart hiding, how dream the products of heart foul
     with egotism and fear?
Heart's dream, the spaces holding you are so indistinct and the hurt place
     you lurk so tender,
that even in dream membranes veil and distort you, only fancy and
     falsehood hint where you are.
How can I dream the stripping away of the petrified membranes muffling
     the tremulous heart?
I reach towards the heart and attain only heart's stores of timidity, self-
     hatred, and blame;
the heart which I don't dare bring to my zone of knowledge for fear it
     will shame me again,
afflict me again with its pettiness, coyness, its sham zeal, false pity, and
     false pride.
Dream of my heart, am I only able to dream illusions of you that touch
     me with pity or pride?
How dream the heart's sorrow to redeem what it contains beyond its self-
     defense and disdain?
How forgive heart when the part of me that beholds heart swells so in
     its pride and contempt?
Trying to dream the dream of the heart, I hide myself from it, I veil my
     failures and shame.
Heart, ever unworthy of you, lost in you, will I ever truly dream you,
     or dream beyond you?

Room

I wanted to take up room. What a strange dream! I wanted to take up as
      much room as I could,
to swell up, enlarge, crowd into a corner all the others in the dream with
      me, but why?
Something to do with love, it felt like, but what love needs more volume
      than it has?
Lust, then: its limitlessness, the lure of its ineluctable renewal—but this
      came before lust.
Fear? Yes, the others were always more real than I was, more concrete,
      emphatic: why not fear?
Though I knew that this was my dream, they were the given and I the
      eccentric, wobbling variable.
A dubious plasma, drifting among them, self-consciously sidling, flowing,
      ebbing among them,
no wonder my atoms would boil, trying to gel, and no wonder I'd some-
      times resent them,
brood on them, trying to understand what they were, what my connection
      to them really was.
Sometimes I'd think the point of the dream was to find what of me was
      embodied in them.
What I was with them, though, what they finally were in themselves, I
      hardly could tell.
Sometimes they seemed beasts; I could see them only as beasts, captives
      of hunger and fear.
Sometimes they were angels, nearly on fire, embracing, gleaming with
      grace, gratitude, praise.
But when their lips touched, were they kissing, or gnawing the warmth
      from a maw?
So much threatening pain to each other, so much pain accomplished:
      no surprise I'd think beasts.
But still, I loved them; I wasn't just jealous of them, I loved them, was
      of them, and, more,
I'd grown somehow to know in the dream that part of my love meant
      accounting for them.

Account for them: how, though, why? Did they account for each other, would they for me?

That wasn't what the dream meant to be now; I loved them, I wasn't to ask if they loved me.

The fear, the loving and being loved, the accounting for and the wish to had all become one.

Dream, where have you brought me? What a strange dream! Who would have thought to be here?

Beasts, angels, taking up room, the ways of duty and love: what next, dream, where now?

History

I have escaped in the dream; I was in danger, at peril, at immediate,
   furious, frightening risk,
but I deftly evaded the risk, eluded the danger, I conned peril to think
   I'd gone that way,
then I went this, then this way again, over the bridges of innocence, into
   the haven of sorrow.
I was so shrewd in my moment of risk, so cool: I was as guileful as though
   I were guilty,
sly, devious, cunning, though I'd done nothing in truth but be who I
   was where I was
when the dream conceived me as a threat I wasn't, possessed of a power
   I'd never had,
though I had found enough strength to flee and the guileful wherewithal
   to elude and be free.
I have escaped and survived, but as soon as I think it it starts again, I'm
   hounded again:
no innocence now, no unlikeliest way, only this frenzied combing of the
   countries of mind
where I always believed I'd find safety and solace but where now are
   confusion and fear
and a turmoil so total that all I have known or might know drags me
   with it towards chaos.
That, in this space I inhabit, something fearsome is happening, headlong,
   with an awful momentum,
is never in doubt, but that's all I can say—no way even to be sure if I'm
   victim or oppressor;
absurd after all this not to know if I'm subject or object, scapegoat,
   perpetrator, or prey.
The dream is of beings like me, assembled, surrounded, herded like
   creatures, driven, undone.
And beings like me, not more like me but like me, assemble and herd
   them, us; undo us.
No escape now, no survival: captured, subjugated, undone, we all move
   through dreams of negation.

Subject, object, dream doesn't care; accumulate or subtract, self as solace, self-blame.

Thou shalt, thou shalt not; thus do I, thus I do not: dream is indifferent, bemused, abstracted.

Formulation, abstraction; assembly, removal: the dream detached; exaltation, execration, denial.

The Gap

So often and with such cruel fascination I have dreamed the implacable
     void that contains dream.
The space there, the silence, the scrawl of trajectories tracked, traced,
     and let go;
the speck of matter in non-matter; sphere, swing, the puff of agglutinate
     loose-woven tissue;
the endless pull of absence on self, the sad molecule of the self in its
     chunk of duration;
the desolate grain, flake, fragment of mind that thinks when the mind
     thinks it's thinking.
So often, too, with equal absorption, I have dreamed the end of it all:
     mind, matter, void.
I'm appalled, but I do it again, I dream it again, it comes uncalled for
     but it comes, always,
rising perhaps out of the fearful demands consciousness makes for linkage,
     coherence, congruence,
connection to something beyond, even if dread: mystery exponentially
     functioned to dread.
Again, premonitions of silence, the swoop through a gulf that might be
     inherent in mind
as though mind bore in its matter its own end and the annulment of
     everything else.
Somehow I always return in the dream from the end, from the mean-
     ingless, the mesh of despair,
but what if I don't once, what if the corrections fail once and I can't
     recover the thread
that leads back from that night beyond night that absorbs night as night
     absorbs innocent day?
The whole of being untempered by self, the great selves beyond self all
     wholly wound out;
sense neutered, knowledge betrayed: what if this is the real end of dream,
     facing the darkness
and subjecting the self yet again to imperious laws of doubt and denial
     which are never repealed?

How much can I do this, how often rejuvenate and redeem with such
partial, imperfect belief?
So often, by something like faith, I'm brought back in the dream; but
this, too; so often this, too.

The Knot

Deciphering and encoding, to translate, fabricate, revise; the abstract star,
the real star;
crossing over boundaries we'd never known were there until we found
ourselves beyond them.
A fascination first: this was why the dream existed, so our definitions
would be realized.
Then more than fascination as we grasped how dream could infiltrate
the mundane with its radiance.
There'd be no mundane anymore: wholly given to the dream, our de-
bilitating skepticisms overcome,
we'd act, or would be acted on—the difference, if there'd been one,
would have been annulled—
with such purity of motive and such temperate desire that outcome would
result from inspiration
with the same illumination that the notion of creation brings when it
first comes upon us.
No question now of fabricating less ambiguous futures, no trying to recast
recalcitrant beginnings.
It would be another empire of determination, in which all movement
would be movement towards—
mergings, joinings—and in which existence would be generated from
the qualities of our volition:
intention flowing outward into form and back into itself in intricate
threadings and weavings,
intuitions shaped as logically as crystal forms in rock, a linkage at the
incandescent core,
knots of purpose we would touch into as surely as we touch the rippling
lattice of a song.
No working out of what we used to call identity; our consummations
would consist of acts,
of participating in a consciousness that wouldn't need, because it grew
from such pure need,
acknowledgment or subject: we'd be held in it, always knowing there
were truths beyond it.

Cleansed even of our appetite for bliss, we'd only want to know the ground of our new wonder,

and we wouldn't be surprised to find that it survived where we'd known it had to all along,

in all for which we'd blamed ourselves, repented and corrected, and never for a moment understood.

The Fear

In my dream of unspecific anxiety, nothing is what it should be, nothing
    acts as it should;
everything shifts, shudders, won't hold still long enough for me to name
    or constrain it.
The fear comes with no premonition, no flicker in the daily surges and
    currents of dream.
Momentums, inertias, then logic distends, distorts, bends in convulsive
    postures of scorn.
All I hold dear rushes away in magnetic repulsion to me, ravaged as
    though by a storm,
but I know that I myself am the storm, I am the force that daunts,
    threatens, rages, repels.
I am like time, I gather the things of creation and drive them out from
    me towards an abyss.
All I call beauty is ravaged, transcendence hauled back in a gust to
    corporeal swarm.
I never believe that the part of me which is fear can raze all the rest with
    such fury,
even the flesh is depleted, forsaken; I'm no longer spirit or flesh but lost
    within both,
negated, forlorn, a thing the dream can capture and propel through itself
    any way it desires.
Nothing to hope for now but more concrete fears that at least might
    reveal their reason.
Nothing to dream but silence and forgetting; everything failing, even the
    wanting to be.

You

Such longing, such urging, such warmth towards, such force towards,
     so much ardor and desire;
to touch, touch into, hold, hold against, to feel, feel against and long
     towards again,
as though the longing, urge, and warmth were ends in themselves, the
     increase of themselves,
the force towards, the ardor and desire, focused, increased, the incar-
     nation of themselves.
All this in the body of dream, all in the substance of dream; allure,
     attraction, and need,
the force so consumed and rapt in its need that dream might have evolved
     it from itself,
except the ardor urges always towards the other, towards you, and without
     you it decays,
becomes vestige, reflex, the defensive attempt to surmount instinctual
     qualms and misgivings.
No qualms now, no misgivings; no hesitancy or qualifications in longing
     towards you;
no frightened wish to evolve ideals to usurp qualm, fear or misgiving,
     not any longer.
The longing towards you sure now, ungeneralized, certain, the urge now
     towards you in yourself,
your own form of nearness, the surface of desire multiplied in the need
     that urges from you,
your longing, your urging, the force and the warmth from you, the sure
     ardor blazing in you.

To Listen

In the dream of death where I listen, the voices of the dream keep
   diminishing, fading away.
The dead are speaking, my dead are speaking, what they say seems urgent,
   to me, to themselves,
but as I try to capture more clearly what I heard just moments ago, the
   voices ebb and it's lost;
what's more, my impatience to know what was said seems to drive it
   further out of my ken.
In the dream of death where I listen, I keep thinking my dead have a
   message for me:
maybe they'll tell me at last why they must always die in the dream, live,
   die, die again.
I still can't hear what they say, though; I force my senses into the silence
   but nothing is there.
Sometimes I listen so hard I think what I'm waiting to hear must already
   have been spoken,
it's here, its echo surrounds me, I just have to learn to bring it more
   clearly within me
and I'll know at last what I never thought I would know about death and
   the dead and the speech
of affection the dead speak that stays on in the sentient space between
   living and after.
For the dead speak from affection, dream says, there's kindness in the
   voices of the dead.
I listen again, but I still hear only fragments of the elaborate discourse
   the dead speak;
when I try to capture its gist more is effaced, there are only faded words
   strewn on the page
of my soul that won't rest from its need to have what it thinks it can have
   from the dead.
Something is in me like greed now, I can't stop trying to tear the silence
   away from the voices,
I tear at the actual voices, though I know what the dead bring us is not
   to be held,

that the wanting to hold it is just what condemns dream to this pained,
    futile listening,
is what brings dream finally to its end, in silence, in want, in believing
    it's lost,
only for now, my dream thinks, at least let it be only for now, my forsaken
    dream thinks,
what the dead brought, what the dead found in their kind, blurred, weary
    voices to bring.

The Covenant

In my unlikeliest dream, my dead are with me again, companions again,
    in an ordinary way;
nothing of major moment to accomplish, no stains to cleanse, no oaths
    or debts to redeem:
my dead are serene, composed, as though they'd known all along how
    this would be.
Only I look aslant, only I brood and fret, marvel; only I have to know
    what this miracle is:
I'm awed, I want to embrace my newly found dead, to ask why they had
    to leave me so abruptly.
In truth, I think, I want pity from them, for my being bereft, for my
    grief and my pain.
But my dead will have none of my sorrow, of my asking how they came
    to be here again.
They anoint me with their mild regard and evidence only the need to
    continue, go on
in a dream that's almost like life in how only the plainest pastimes of
    love accumulate worth.
Cured of all but their presence, they seem only to want me to grasp their
    new way of being.
At first I feel nothing, then to my wonder and perhaps, too, the wonder
    of the dead,
I sense an absence in them, of will, of anything like will, as though will
    in the soul
had for the dead been all given over, transfigured, to humility, resig-
    nation, submission.
I know without knowing how that the dead can remember the movements
    of will, thought willing,
the gaze fixed at a distance that doesn't exist, the mind in its endless war
    with itself—
those old cravings—but the striving to will themselves from themselves
    is only a dream,
the dead know what death has brought is all they need now because all
    else was already possessed,

all else was a part of the heart as it lived, in what it had seen and what
it had suffered,
in the love it had hardly remarked coming upon it, so taken it was with
its work of volition.
I can hardly believe that so little has to be lost to find such good fortune
in death,
and then, as I dream again the suspensions of will I'm still only just able
to dream,
I suddenly know I've beheld death myself, and instead of the terror, the
flexions of fear,
the repulsion, recoil, impatience to finish, be done with the waiting once
and for all,
I feel the same surge of acceptance, patience, and joy I felt in my dead
rising in me:
I know that my dead have brought what I've restlessly waited all the life
of the dream for.
I wait in joy as they give themselves to the dream once again; waiting,
I'm with them again.

Light

Always in the dream I seemed conscious of myself having the dream even
    as I dreamed it.
Even now, the dream moving towards light, the field of light flowing
    gently towards me,
I watch myself dreaming, I watch myself dreaming and watching, I watch
    both watchers together.
It almost seems that this is what dream is about, to think what happens
    as it's happening.
Still, aren't there disturbing repercussions in being in such an active
    relation with dream?
What about nightmare, for instance; nightmare is always lurking there
    out at the edges,
it's part of dream's definition: how be so involved in the intimate workings
    of dream
without being an accomplice of nightmare, a portion of its cause or even
    its actual cause?
Doesn't what comes to me have to be my fault, and wouldn't the alter-
    native be more troubling still—
that I might *not* be the one engendering this havoc, that I'm only allowed
    to think so,
that the nightmare itself, hauling me through its vales of anguish, is the
    operative force?
What do I mean by nightmare itself, though? Wouldn't that imply a
    mind here besides mine?
But how else explain all the *care*, first to involve me, then to frighten
    me out of my wits?
Mustn't something with other agendas be shaping the dream; don't all
    the enticements and traps
suggest an intention more baleful than any I'd have for visiting such
    mayhem on myself?
And if this isn't the case, wouldn't the alternative be as bad; that each
    element of the dream
would contain its own entailment so that what came next would just do
    so for no special reason?

How frivolous dream would be, then: either way, though, so much
   subjugation, so little choice.
Either way, isn't the real nightmare my having so little power, *even over
   my own consciousness?*
Sometimes, when I arrive in dream here, when I arrive nearly over-
   whelmed with uncertainty here,
I feel a compulsion to renounce what so confounds me, to abdicate,
   surrender, but to what?
I don't even know if my despair might not be another deception the
   devious dream is proposing.
At last, sometimes, perhaps driven to this, perhaps falling upon it in
   exhaustion or resignation,
I try to recapture how I once dreamed, innocently, with no thought of
   being beside or beyond:
I imagine myself in that healing accord I still somehow believe must
   precede or succeed dream.
My vigilance never flags, though; I behold the infernal beholder, I behold
   the uncanny beheld,
this mind streaming through me, its turbulent stillness, its murmur,
   inexorable, beguiling.

5

Helen

More voice was in her cough tonight: its first harsh, stripping sound
    would weaken abruptly,
and he'd hear the voice again, not hers, unrecognizable, its notes from
    somewhere else,
someone saying something they didn't seem to want to say, in a tongue
    they hadn't mastered,
or a singer, diffident and hesitating, searching for a place to start an
    unfamiliar melody.

Its pitch was gentle, almost an interrogation, intimate, a plea, a moan,
    almost sexual,
but he could hear assertion, too, a straining from beneath, a forcing at
    the withheld consonant,
and he realized that she was holding back, trying with great effort not to
    cough again,
to change the spasm to a tone instead and so avert the pain that lurked
    out at the stress.

Then he heard her lose her almost-word, almost-song: it became a groan,
    the groan a gasp,
the gasp a sigh of desperation, then the cough rasped everything away,
    everything was cough now,
he could hear her shuddering, the voice that for a moment seemed the
    gentlest part of her,
choked down, effaced, abraded, taken back, as all of her was being taken
    from him now.

2

In the morning she was standing at the window; he lay where he was
    and quietly watched her.

A sound echoed in from somewhere, she turned to listen, and he was
shocked at how she moved:
not *enough* moved, just her head, pivoting methodically, the mechanisms
slowed nearly to a halt,
as though she was afraid to jar herself with the contracting tendons and
skeletal leverings.

A flat, cool, dawn light washed in on her: how pale her skin was, how
dull her tangled hair.
So much of her had burned away, and what was left seemed draped
listlessly upon her frame.
It was her eye that shocked him most, though; he could only see her
profile, and the eye in it,
without fire or luster, was strangely isolated from her face, and even from
her character.

For the time he looked at her, the eye existed not as her eye, his wife's,
his beloved's eye,
but as *an* eye, an object, so emphatic, so pronounced, it was separate
both from what it saw
and from who saw with it: it could have been a creature's eye, a member
of that larger class
which simply indicated sight and not that essence which her glance had
always brought him.

It came to him that though she hadn't given any sign, she knew that he
was watching her.
He was saddened that she'd tolerate his seeing her as she was now, weak,
disheveled, haggard.
He felt that they were both involved, him watching, her letting him, in
a depressing indiscretion:
she'd always, after all their time together, only offered him the images
she thought he wanted.

She'd known how much he needed beauty, how much presumed it as
the elemental of desire.
The loveliness that illuminated her had been an engrossing narrative his
spirit fed on;

he entered it and flowed out again renewed for having touched within
    and been a part of it.
In his meditations on her, he'd become more complicated, fuller, more
    essential to himself.

It was to her beauty he'd made love at first, she was there within its
    captivating light,
but was almost secondary, as though she was just the instance of some
    overwhelming generality.
She herself was shy before it; she, too, as unassumingly as possible was
    testing this abstraction
which had taken both of them into its sphere, rendering both subservient
    to its serene enormity.

As their experience grew franker, and as she learned to move more
    confidently towards her core,
became more overtly active in elaborating needs and urges, her beauty
    still came first.
In his memory, it seemed to him that they'd unsheathed her from the
    hazes of their awe,
as though her unfamiliar, fiery, famished nakedness had been disclosed
    as much to her as him.

She'd been grateful to him, and that gratitude became in turn another
    fact of his desire.
Her beauty had acknowledged him, allowed him in its secret precincts,
    let him be its celebrant,
an implement of its luxurious materiality, and though he remained as-
    tonished by it always,
he fulfilled the tasks it demanded of him, his devotions reinvigorated and
    renewed.

3

In the deepest sense, though, he'd never understood what her beauty was
    or really meant.

95

If you only casually beheld her, there were no fanfares, you were taken
by no immolating ecstasies.
It amused him sometimes seeing other men at first not really understand-
ing what they saw;
no one dared to say it, but he could feel them holding back their dis-
appointment or disbelief.

Was this Helen, mythic Helen, this female, fleshed like any other, im-
perfect and approachable?
He could understand: he himself, when he'd first seen her, hadn't really;
he'd even thought,
before he'd registered her spirit and intelligence, before her laughter's
melodies had startled him—
if only one could alter such and such, improve on this or that: he hardly
could believe it now.

But so often he'd watched others hear her speak, or laugh, look at her
again, and fall in love,
as puzzled as he'd been at the time they'd wasted while their raptures of
enchantment took.
Those who hadn't ever known her sometimes spoke of her as though she
were his thing, his toy,
but that implied something static in her beauty, and she was surely just
the opposite of that.

If there was little he'd been able to explain of what so wonderfully ab-
sorbed him in her,
he knew it was a movement and a process, that he was taken towards
and through her beauty,
touched by it but even more participating in its multiplicities, the rev-
elations of its grace.
He felt himself becoming real in her, tangible, as though before he'd
only half existed.

Sometimes he would even feel it wasn't really him being brought to such
unlikely fruition.
Absurd that anyone so coarse and ordinary should be in touch with such
essential mystery:

something else, beyond him, something he would never understand,
used him for its affirmations.
What his reflections came to was something like humility, then a gratitude
of his own.

4

The next night her cough was worse, with a harsher texture, the spasms
came more rapidly,
and they'd end with a deep, complicated emptying, like the whining
flattening of a bagpipe.
The whole event seemed to need more labor: each cough sounded more
futile than the last,
as though the effort she'd made and the time lost making it had added
to the burden of illness.

Should he go to her? He felt she'd moved away from him, turning more
intently towards herself.
Her sickness absorbed her like a childbirth; she seemed almost like some-
one he didn't know.
There'd been so many Helens, the first timid girl, then the sensual Helen
of their years together,
then the last, whose grace had been more intricate and difficult to know
and to exult in.

How childishly frightened he'd always been by beauty's absence, by its
destruction or perversity.
For so long he let himself be tormented by what he knew would have to
happen to her.
He'd seen the old women as their thighs and buttocks bloated, then
withered and went slack,
as their dugs dried, skin dried, legs were sausaged with the veins that rose
like kelp.

He'd tried to overcome himself, to feel compassion towards them, but,
perhaps because of her,

he'd felt only a shameful irritation, as though they were colluding in
their loss.
Whether they accepted what befell them, even, he would think, gladly
acquiescing to it,
or fought it, with all their sad and valiant unguents, dyes, and ointments,
was equally degrading.

His own body had long ago become a ruin, but beauty had never been
a part of what he was.
What would happen to his lust, and to his love, when time came to
savage and despoil her?
He already felt his will deserting him; for a long time, though, nothing
touched or dulled her:
perhaps she really was immortal, maybe his devotion kept her from the
steely rakings of duration.

Then, one day, something at her jowls; one day her hips; one day the
flesh at her elbows . . .
One day, one day, one day he looked at her and knew that what he'd
feared so was upon them.
He couldn't understand how all his worst imaginings had come to pass
without his noticing.
Had he all this while been blind, or had he not wanted to acknowledge
what he'd dreaded?

He'd been gazing at her then; in her wise way, she'd looked back at him,
and touched him,
and he knew she'd long known what was going on in him: another
admiration took him,
then another fire, and that simply, he felt himself closer to her: there'd
been no trial,
nothing had been lost, of lust, of love, and something he'd never dreamed
would be was gained.

5

With her in the darkness now, not even touching her, he sensed her
fever's suffocating dryness.

He couldn't, however much he wanted to, not let himself believe she
   was to be no more.
And there was nothing he could do for her even if she'd let him; he tried
   to calm himself.
Her cough was hollow, soft, almost forgiving, ebbing slowly through the
   volumes of her thorax.

He could almost hear that world as though from in her flesh: the current
   of her breath,
then her breastbone, ribs, and spine, taking on the cough's vibrations,
   giving back their own.
Then he knew precisely how she was within herself as well, he was with
   her as he'd never been:
he'd unmoored in her, cast himself into the night of her, and perceived
   her life with her.

All she'd lived through, all she'd been and done, he could feel accu-
   mulated in this instant.
The impressions and sensations, feelings, dreams, and memories were
   tearing loose in her,
had disconnected from each other and randomly begun to float, collide,
   collapse, entangle;
they were boiling in a matrix of sheer chance, suspended in a purely
   mental universe of possibility.

He knew that what she was now to herself, what she remembered, might
   not in truth have ever been.
Who, then, was she now, who was the person she had been, if all she
   was, all he still so adored,
was muddled, addled, mangled: what of her could be repository now,
   the place where she existed?
When everything was shorn from her, what within this flux of fragments
   still stayed her?

He knew then what he had to do: he was so much of her now and she
   of him that she was his,
her consciousness and memory both his, he would will her into him,
   keep her from her dissolution.
All the wreckage of her fading life, its shattered hours taken in this fearful
   flood,

its moments unrecoverable leaves twirling in a gust across a waste of loss, he drew into himself,

and held her, kept her, all the person she had been was there within his sorrow and his longing:
it didn't matter what delirium had captured her, what of her was being lacerated, rent,
his pain had taken on a power, his need for her became a force that he could focus on her;
there was something in him like triumph as he shielded her within the absolute of his affection.

Then he couldn't hold it, couldn't keep it, it was all illusion, a confection of his sorrow:
there wasn't room within the lenses of his mortal being to contain what she had been,
to do justice to a single actual instant of her life and soul, a single moment of her mind,
and he released her then, let go of this diminished apparition he'd created from his fear.

But still, he gave himself to her, without moving moved to her: she was still his place of peace.
He listened for her breath: was she still here with him, did he have her that way, too?
He heard only the flow of the silent darkness, but he knew now that in it they'd become it,
their shells of flesh and form, the old delusion of their separateness and incompletion, gone.

When one last time he tried to bring her image back, she was as vivid as he'd ever seen her.
What they were together, everything they'd lived, all that seemed so fragile, bound in time,
had come together in him, in both of them: she had entered death, he was with her in it.
Death was theirs, she'd become herself again; her final, searing loveliness had been revealed.

Printed in the United States
47471LVS00003B/238